Is Baptism
Really Necessary?

Is Baptism Really Necessary?

A study from the Scriptures alone

Paul Hainline

NobleMind Press

noblemind.study

NobleMind Press • noblemind.study

All Scripture quotations are from the
New American Standard Bible (NASB).

ISBN: 979-8-9954288-9-3

Contents

*Father, we ask that You open the heart and eyes of
every person who reads these words. Not to our wisdom
— we have none of our own — but to Yours. Let Your
word speak plainly, and give us the honesty and
courage to follow wherever it leads. In the name of
Jesus Christ, amen.*

There is a question that has been asked in churches, Bible studies, and living room conversations for generations: *Is baptism really necessary?*

The answer is not complicated. But it does require honesty — the willingness to set aside what we have been taught by men and look at what the Scriptures actually say. Not what we want them to say. Not what we have always assumed they say. What they *actually* say.

I know what I am asking. For many of you, your faith was inherited. It was handed down by parents and grandparents and generations before them — people you love, people you trust, people who are no longer here to ask. And the thought of questioning what they believed feels like a betrayal of the people who gave it to you.

But ask yourself this: if they were wrong — if they believed something that was not what the Scriptures teach — what would they want for you? Would they want you to continue in their error out of loyalty? Or would they want you to know the truth? Every loving parent and grandparent who has ever lived would give the same answer. They would want more truth for you, not less. Honor them by being honest with the text. That is not betrayal. That is the deepest kind of faithfulness.

Let us look together.

. . .

The Command

Before we examine anything else, we must start here: Jesus commanded it.

Jesus said, *"I will build **My** church"* (Matthew 16:18). Not someone else's church. *His* church. Built by *Him*, on *His* terms, according to *His* commands. And in the final words He spoke to His apostles before ascending to the Father, Jesus said:

> *"Go therefore and make disciples of all the nations, baptizing them in the name of the Father and the Son and the Holy Spirit, teaching them to observe all that I commanded you; and lo, I am with you always, even to the end of the age."*
>
> — Matthew 28:19–20

And in the Gospel of Mark:

> *"He who has believed and has been baptized shall be saved; but he who has disbelieved shall be condemned."*
>
> — Mark 16:16

Read that again. "He who has believed *and has been baptized* shall be saved." Not "he who has believed shall be saved and may also consider being baptized at some point." Belief and baptism are joined together in the Lord's own words. On what authority does anyone separate what Jesus joined?

This is not a suggestion. This is not an invitation to consider a symbolic gesture at your convenience. This is a command from the head of the church. And the question every honest person must ask is: *If Jesus commanded it, how can anyone call it unnecessary?*

. . .

Born of Water and the Spirit

Before the cross, before the Great Commission, Jesus had already spoken of this. In His conversation with Nicodemus — a Pharisee, a ruler of the Jews, a man who came to Jesus by night — Jesus said:

> *"Truly, truly, I say to you, unless one is born again he cannot see the kingdom of God."*
>
> — John 3:3

Nicodemus was confused. He asked how a man could be born a second time. And Jesus answered:

> *"Truly, truly, I say to you, unless one is born of water and the Spirit he cannot enter into the kingdom of God."*
>
> — John 3:5

Born of water and the Spirit. Not one or the other. Both. Jesus was telling Nicodemus — and every person who would ever read these words — that entering the kingdom of God requires a birth of water and Spirit. And the apostles, who heard Jesus teach and were sent out to preach His gospel, understood exactly what He meant. Their preaching — and the response of every convert in the book of Acts — makes that understanding unmistakable.

. . .

What Baptism Is

Before we go further, we must be clear about what baptism actually is — because what many practice today bears little resemblance to what the New Testament describes.

The English word "baptism" is not a translation. It is a transliteration — the Greek word *baptizo* carried over into English with its spelling changed but its meaning left behind. The Greek word means to immerse, to submerge, to plunge beneath. It does not mean to sprinkle. It does not mean to pour. It means to put completely under.

And the Scriptures confirm this in the way they describe it. Paul wrote:

> *"Therefore we have been buried with Him through baptism into death, so that as Christ was raised from the dead through the glory of the Father, so we too might walk in newness of life."*
>
> — Romans 6:4

Buried. Not sprinkled on. Not dabbed. *Buried.* You do not bury someone by scattering a handful of dirt on their head. You bury someone by putting them completely under. Baptism is a burial in water and a resurrection out of it — the old man goes down, the new man comes up. That is the picture Paul paints, and it only makes sense as full, complete immersion.

When Philip baptized the Ethiopian eunuch, the text says *"they both went down into the water"* and then *"came up out of the water"* (Acts 8:38–39). They did not stand on the bank while Philip sprinkled him. They went down into the water together.

When Jesus Himself was baptized by John, He *"came up immediately from the water"* (Matthew 3:16). He was in the water. He came up out of it.

And this is why John was baptizing at a specific location: *"John also was baptizing in Aenon near Salim, because there was much water there"* (John 3:23). If baptism were sprinkling or pouring, any small vessel of water would do. John needed *much water* — because baptism requires enough water to immerse a person completely.

As for infant baptism — there is no command for it, no example of it, and no hint of it anywhere in the New Testament. Baptism requires belief: *"He who has believed and has been baptized shall be saved"* (Mark 16:16). It requires repentance: *"Repent, and each of you be baptized"* (Acts 2:38). An infant can neither believe, nor repent, nor confess Christ — and an infant has no need to. Baptism is for the forgiveness of sins, and an infant has committed no sin. Sin is not inherited. Sin is a deliberate act of transgression — *"sin is lawlessness"* (1 John 3:4) — and a child who has never known the difference between right and wrong has committed no transgression. Every conversion in the book of Acts involves a person who heard the gospel, believed it, and chose to be baptized. Baptism is a conscious act of obedient faith — and it always has been.

· · ·

What the Apostles Taught

If baptism were optional, we would expect the apostles to treat it that way. But they did not. Not once.

Peter, on the day of Pentecost — the very first gospel sermon ever preached after the resurrection — told the crowd:

> *"Repent, and each of you be baptized in the name of Jesus Christ for the forgiveness of your sins; and you will receive the gift of the Holy Spirit."*
> — Acts 2:38

"For the forgiveness of your sins." Not as a symbol of forgiveness already received. *For* the forgiveness of sins. That is what the word says.

And Peter, decades later, wrote:

> *"Corresponding to that, baptism now saves you — not the removal of dirt from the flesh, but an appeal to God for a good conscience — through the resurrection of Jesus Christ."*
>
> — 1 Peter 3:21

"Baptism now saves you." Peter even anticipated the objection — he clarified that he was not talking about the physical act of washing. He was talking about the appeal to God, the act of faith, that takes place in baptism. And he said it *saves you*. Could the language be any clearer?

Paul wrote to the Romans:

> *"Or do you not know that all of us who have been baptized into Christ Jesus have been baptized into His death? Therefore we have been buried with Him through baptism into death, so that as Christ was raised from the dead through the glory of the Father, so we too might walk in newness of life."*
>
> — Romans 6:3–4

Baptism is where a person is buried with Christ and raised with Him. The old life dies. The new life begins.

To the Galatians:

"For all of you who were baptized into Christ have clothed yourselves with Christ."

— Galatians 3:27

How does one get "into Christ"? By being baptized into Him. How does one put on Christ? Through baptism. There is no ambiguity here. And this matters more than most people realize, because of what Paul wrote to the Ephesians:

"Blessed be the God and Father of our Lord Jesus Christ, who has blessed us with every spiritual blessing in the heavenly places in Christ."

— Ephesians 1:3

Every spiritual blessing is in Christ. Every one. And the only two places in all of Scripture that tell you how to get *into* Christ — Romans 6:3 and Galatians 3:27 — both say the same thing: you are baptized into Him. If every blessing is in Christ, and the only way into Christ is through baptism, then to reject baptism is to remain outside of where every spiritual blessing resides.

To the Colossians:

"Having been buried with Him in baptism, in which you were also raised up with Him through faith in the working of God, who raised Him from the dead."

— Colossians 2:12

And Paul reminded the Ephesians that there is:

"One Lord, one faith, one baptism."

— Ephesians 4:5

One baptism — placed alongside one Lord and one faith. Not optional. Not secondary. Essential.

To the Corinthians:

> *"For by one Spirit we were all baptized into one body, whether Jews or Greeks, whether slaves or free, and we were all made to drink of one Spirit."*
>
> — 1 Corinthians 12:13

And to Titus:

> *"He saved us, not on the basis of deeds which we have done in righteousness, but according to His mercy, by the washing of regeneration and renewing by the Holy Spirit."*
>
> — Titus 3:5

The washing of regeneration. The new birth. The same thing Jesus told Nicodemus: born of water and the Spirit.

And when **Ananias** came to Saul of Tarsus — the man who would become the apostle Paul — he said:

> *"Now why do you delay? Get up and be baptized, and wash away your sins, calling on His name."*
>
> — Acts 22:16

Every apostle. Every letter. Every sermon. The same message: baptism is where sins are washed away, where a person is buried with Christ and raised to walk in newness of life, where one enters the body of Christ. Not one of them called it optional. Not one of them called it merely symbolic.

. . .

What the Early Church Did — Every Single Time

If the teaching is not convincing enough, look at what they *did*. The book of Acts records conversion after conversion. And in every single one, baptism is present. There are no exceptions.

Pentecost (Acts 2:38–47) — Peter preached, three thousand souls were "pierced to the heart," and Peter told them to repent and be baptized. That day, three thousand were baptized. And then the text tells us who did what next: *"And the Lord was adding to their number day by day those who were being saved"* (Acts 2:47). Not a committee. Not a vote. Not a preacher declaring them saved. The *Lord* added them — to *His* church, the one *He* said He would build. And He added them after they obeyed His command to be baptized.

The Samaritans (Acts 8:12–13) — When they believed Philip's preaching about the kingdom of God and the name of Jesus Christ, "they were being baptized, men and women alike."

The Ethiopian Eunuch (Acts 8:35–39) — Philip "preached Jesus to him." That is all the text says — he preached Jesus. And as they traveled down the road, the eunuch saw water and said, *"Look! Water! What prevents me from being baptized?"*

Think about what that tells us. Philip preached Jesus, and the eunuch's immediate response was to look for water. Preaching Jesus *includes* preaching baptism — or the eunuch would never have known to ask. He did not ask about a prayer. He did not ask about a moment of personal acceptance. He saw water and asked to be baptized. Because that is what preaching Christ looks like. And when they came up out of the water, the text says *"he went on his way rejoicing"* (Acts 8:39). Not before baptism. After. The rejoicing came when his obedience was complete.

Saul of Tarsus (Acts 9:1–18; 22:6–16) — This conversion deserves careful attention, because it dismantles every argument that belief alone is sufficient.

Saul encountered Jesus on the road to Damascus. He saw the risen Lord. He heard His voice. He asked, *"Who are You, Lord?"* and was told, *"I am Jesus whom you are persecuting."* From that moment, Saul believed. There is no question about it — he had met the Lord face to face.

And what did Saul do? He went into the city. He fasted. He prayed. For three days he neither ate nor drank. If ever a man demonstrated belief, repentance, and earnest prayer, it was Saul during those three days.

But he was still in his sins.

When Ananias arrived, he did not say, "Good news — you were saved on the road." He did not say, "Your faith has already taken care of it." He said: *"Now why do you delay? Get up and be baptized, and wash away your sins, calling on His name"* (Acts 22:16).

Wash away your sins. *After* believing. *After* fasting. *After* praying. Saul's sins were still there — and they remained there until he was baptized. If belief alone were enough, Saul would have been saved on the road. If prayer alone were enough, Saul would have been saved during those three days. But he was not. He was told to be baptized and wash away his sins. And he did.

Cornelius and His Household (Acts 10:44–48) — Cornelius is a remarkable case, and it requires understanding what happened and why. While Peter was still speaking, the Holy Spirit fell upon Cornelius and his household. They spoke in tongues. They praised God. And the Jewish Christians who had come with Peter were amazed.

Why did this happen? For the same reason the Holy Spirit fell on the apostles at Pentecost. At Pentecost, the Spirit came upon the apostles so the crowd could see that these men spoke by the power of God — they spoke in real languages that each listener understood in his own tongue (Acts 2:6–8), not unintelligible speech. It was a sign to the people that God was behind what was happening. With Cornelius, the Spirit fell for the same reason — not to save Cornelius, but to show Peter and the Jews with him that God was opening the door to the Gentiles. Peter himself explained this later: *"The Holy Spirit fell upon them just as He did upon us at the beginning"* (Acts 11:15). It was God's testimony that the gospel was for all people, not Jews alone.

And Peter's response was not, "Well, they clearly don't need baptism now." His response was:

> *"Surely no one can refuse the water for these to be baptized who have received the Holy Spirit just as we did, can he?"*
> — Acts 10:47

And he *ordered* them to be baptized. Even after receiving the Holy Spirit directly — a miraculous, unmistakable sign from God — baptism was still required. The Spirit confirmed that Gentiles were welcome. Baptism is what brought them into Christ. Who could deny them the water? And who would dare deny that it was necessary?

Lydia (Acts 16:14–15) — The Lord opened her heart to respond to the things spoken by Paul. And she was baptized, along with her household.

The Philippian Jailer (Acts 16:30–33) — The jailer cried out, *"What must I do to be saved?"* Paul and Silas spoke the word of the Lord to him. And he was baptized *"that very hour of the night"* — he and all his household.

That very hour of the night. Not the next morning. Not the following Sunday. That hour. In the middle of the night. Why? Because baptism is not a ceremony to be scheduled. It is the moment sins are washed away. And that cannot wait.

The Corinthians (Acts 18:8) — "Many of the Corinthians when they heard were believing and being baptized." Believing *and* being baptized. Together. Inseparable.

The Disciples at Ephesus (Acts 19:1–5) — Paul found disciples who had been baptized only with John's baptism. They had not even heard of the Holy Spirit. And Paul had them baptized again — in the name of the Lord Jesus. If baptism were merely a symbol, why would Paul require it a second time? Because it is not a symbol. It matters *what* baptism and *whose* baptism.

Nine conversions. Nine baptisms. No exceptions. Every single one of them was baptized — immediately, urgently, without delay.

. . .

Where Is the Sinner's Prayer?

In many denominations today, a person who wants to be saved is told to bow their head, close their eyes, and repeat a prayer — the so-called "sinner's prayer." The preacher says, "Just say these words with me," and when the prayer is over, the person is told they are saved.

But where is this prayer in the Bible?

It is not at Pentecost. Peter did not tell three thousand people to bow their heads and repeat after him. He told them to repent and be baptized.

It is not on the road to Gaza. Philip did not lead the Ethiopian eunuch in a prayer. The eunuch saw water and asked to be baptized.

It is not in Damascus. Ananias did not ask Saul to pray a prayer of acceptance — Saul had already been praying for three days. Ananias told him to get up and be baptized and wash away his sins.

It is not in Caesarea. Peter did not lead Cornelius in a prayer. He ordered him to be baptized.

It is not in Philippi. Paul and Silas did not hand the jailer a prayer to recite in the middle of the night. They spoke the word of the Lord to him, and he was baptized that very hour.

It is not anywhere. In nine conversion accounts in the book of Acts, the sinner's prayer appears zero times. Not once. Not in any form. No apostle ever told anyone to "just say this prayer with me." Every single time, without exception, the answer was baptism.

So where did the sinner's prayer come from? Not from Jesus. Not from the apostles. Not from Scripture. It is a human tradition — invented centuries after the New Testament was written — and it has replaced the very thing that Jesus commanded and every apostle preached.

The question every honest person must ask is this: *When the apostles — the men Jesus personally trained and sent — told people to be baptized, on what authority does anyone today replace that with a prayer that appears nowhere in the word of God?*

"What Must I Do?"

There are only two places in the book of Acts where someone asks the apostles, in plain language, what they must do to be saved. And the answers they received — given by two different apostles, in two different cities, to two completely different audiences — are remarkably consistent. More than that, they are a precise application of what Jesus Himself had already commanded.

At Pentecost, the crowd — devout Jews who had just realized they had crucified the Messiah — were pierced to the heart and cried out, *"Brethren, what shall we do?"* (Acts 2:37). These were people who already believed in God. They had just come to believe in Jesus. Faith was already present. So Peter told them the next step: *"Repent, and each of you be baptized in the name of Jesus Christ for the forgiveness of your sins"* (Acts 2:38).

In Philippi, the jailer — a pagan who knew nothing of Jesus — cried out, *"What must I do to be saved?"* (Acts 16:30). He was starting from nothing. So Paul and Silas began at the beginning: *"Believe in the Lord Jesus"* (Acts 16:31). But they did not stop there. The text says they *"spoke the word of the Lord to him,"* and that very hour of the night, he was baptized — he and his entire household (Acts 16:32–33).

Now compare both answers to what Jesus said before He ascended:

"He who has believed and has been baptized shall be saved."

— Mark 16:16

"Go therefore and make disciples of all the nations, baptizing them in the name of the Father and the Son and the Holy Spirit, teaching them to observe all that I commanded you."

— Matthew 28:19–20

Jesus gave the formula: belief and baptism — salvation. And He told His apostles to teach people to observe *all* that He had commanded. Not some. Not the parts that feel comfortable. *All.*

And that is exactly what they did. Peter applied it to people who already believed: repent and be baptized — forgiveness. Paul spoke the word of the Lord to the jailer — *all* of it — and the jailer was baptized that very hour. Philip preached Jesus to the Ethiopian eunuch — and because he taught him to observe *all* that Jesus commanded, the eunuch's immediate response was to look for water (Acts 8:35–36). Peter preached to Cornelius, and when the Spirit confirmed that Gentiles were welcome, Peter *ordered* them to be baptized (Acts 10:48). In every case, the apostles were doing what Jesus told them to do: teaching people to observe all that He had commanded — and what He had commanded included baptism.

These are not three different plans of salvation. They are three expressions of the same one. Jesus stated the requirement. The apostles carried it out. And every time someone asked, *"What must I do?"* — the answer always included baptism. Always.

A Common Objection — and a Simple Answer

Some will point to the second half of Mark 16:16 — *"but he who has disbelieved shall be condemned"* — and note that Jesus did not mention baptism in the condemnation. From this, they conclude that baptism must not be necessary.

But consider the logic of the statement. A doctor might say to his patient, "Take your medicine and eat well, and you will recover. But if you refuse the medicine, you will die." The doctor did not mention food in the second half — but no one would conclude that eating well is therefore unnecessary for recovery. The failure to take the medicine is the *first* and most fundamental failure. A person who refuses to believe has already rejected the foundation — there is no reason to address baptism, because they never got that far.

Jesus did not exclude baptism from the requirement. He simply identified unbelief as the root of condemnation. And the first half of His statement stands exactly as He said it: *"He who has believed and has been baptized shall be saved."*

"But Paul Said He Was Not Sent to Baptize"

Another common objection comes from Paul's first letter to the Corinthians:

> *"For **Christ did not send me to baptize, but to preach the gospel**, not in cleverness of speech, so that the cross of Christ would not be made void."*
>
> — 1 Corinthians 1:17

On the surface, this appears to be Paul himself saying that baptism is not part of the gospel — or at least that it is secondary to it. But the context tells a very different story.

The Corinthian church was divided. Members were aligning themselves with the men who had baptized them — *"I am of Paul," "I am of Apollos," "I am of Cephas"* (1 Corinthians 1:12). Paul was horrified. He asked, *"Was Paul crucified for you? Or were you baptized in the name of Paul?"* (1 Corinthians 1:13). His point was not that baptism is unimportant. His point was that *who performs the baptism* is irrelevant — and that he was glad he had personally baptized only a few of them, so no one could claim to belong to Paul's camp.

And notice: Paul still baptized some of them. He names them — Crispus, Gaius, and the household of Stephanas (1 Corinthians 1:14–16). Why would Paul baptize anyone at all if baptism were unnecessary? And Acts 18:8 tells us what happened when the gospel was first preached in Corinth: *"Many of the Corinthians when they heard were believing and being baptized."* Every one of them was baptized. Paul was simply not the one holding them under the water — and he was grateful for that, given how they had turned baptism into a source of division.

Paul was not diminishing baptism. He was diminishing *himself as the baptizer*. There is a world of difference between saying "I was not sent to be the one baptizing" and "baptism does not matter." Paul made the first statement. He never made the second. In fact, this is the same Paul who wrote that we are *"baptized into Christ"* (Romans 6:3), *"clothed with Christ"* through baptism (Galatians 3:27), and *"buried with Him in baptism"* (Colossians 2:12). To claim that Paul did not believe baptism was essential is to ignore everything else he ever wrote about it.

• • •

Not an Outward Expression of an Inward Grace

One of the most common things said about baptism in denominations today is that it is "an outward expression of an inward grace" — a public declaration of a salvation that has already occurred.

But this phrase appears nowhere in Scripture. Not once. It is a human invention, and the conversions in the book of Acts contradict it directly.

If baptism were merely an outward expression, it could wait. It could be scheduled for a convenient Sunday. It could be postponed until a class is completed or a ceremony is arranged. But the early church did not treat it that way — not once.

The Ethiopian eunuch stopped his chariot on the side of a desert road. The Philippian jailer was baptized in the middle of the night. Saul was told, *"Why do you delay?"* Three thousand were baptized the same day they heard the gospel. In every case, baptism was treated as urgent — because it *was* the moment of salvation, not a reflection of it.

Peter did not say, "Baptism now *represents* your salvation." He said, *"Baptism now saves you"* (1 Peter 3:21). Paul did not say, "You *symbolically* clothed yourselves with Christ." He said, *"All of you who were baptized into Christ have clothed yourselves with Christ"* (Galatians 3:27). Ananias did not say, "Be baptized to show that your sins have already been washed away." He said, *"Be baptized, and wash away your sins"* (Acts 22:16).

The language of Scripture does not support the idea of baptism as a symbol. It supports baptism as the moment of transfer — the moment a person passes from what Paul called "the domain of darkness" into "the kingdom of His beloved Son" (Colossians 1:13).

. . .

"But We Are Saved by Grace, Not Works"

This is perhaps the most frequently cited objection. And it begins with a passage that is absolutely true:

— Ephesians 2:8–9

By grace, through faith, not of works. This is true. But the question that must be asked is: *what works?*

Paul was writing to the Ephesians — a mixed congregation of Jews and Gentiles. The great controversy of the early church was whether Gentile converts had to keep the Law of Moses — circumcision, dietary laws, Sabbath observance, the sacrificial system. This is the context of Paul's letters. When Paul says "not of works," he is talking about works of the Law. He makes this explicit elsewhere:

— Galatians 2:16

Works of the Law. That is what cannot save you. No amount of law-keeping earns salvation. But obedience to the commands of Christ is not the same as works of the Law. And the Scriptures make this distinction clear through examples that no honest reader can miss.

Noah — *"By faith Noah, being warned by God about things not yet seen, in reverence prepared an ark for the salvation of his household"* (Hebrews 11:7). Noah built the ark. He cut the wood. He sealed it with pitch. He labored for years. Was that a "work"? Did his obedience earn his salvation? Or did God save him *when he obeyed*?

Naaman — The Syrian commander was told by Elisha to dip in the Jordan River seven times to be cleansed of his leprosy (2 Kings 5). Naaman was angry at first — he expected something more dramatic. But when he humbled himself and obeyed, dipping seven times, he was healed. Did dipping in the river earn his healing? Or did God heal him *when he obeyed*?

Jericho — *"By faith the walls of Jericho fell down after they had been encircled for seven days"* (Hebrews 11:30). Israel marched around the city. They shouted. The walls fell. Did marching knock the walls down? Did shouting collapse the stone? Or did God act *when they obeyed*?

In every case, God required an act of obedient faith. The act itself did not produce the result. God's power accomplished it. But God chose to act *at the point of obedience*. And baptism is no different. God washes away sins. God transfers a person from darkness to light. But He has chosen to do it *at the point of baptism* — just as He healed Naaman at the point of dipping, and saved Noah at the point of entering the ark, and brought down the walls at the point of the shout.

Obedience has never negated grace. It is the *response* to grace. And anyone who says that obeying Christ's command to be baptized is "adding works to the gospel" must also say that Noah should not have built the ark and Naaman should not have dipped in the river.

. . .

Not by Faith Alone

There is another side to this. Many teach that we are saved by "faith alone." But there is only one place in all of Scripture where the words "faith alone" appear together — and it says the opposite of what most people assume:

> *"You see that a man is justified by works and not by faith alone."*
>
> — James 2:24

Not by faith alone. The only time that phrase appears in the Bible, it is preceded by "not."

James does not contradict Paul. Paul says we are not saved by works of the Law. James says we are not saved by faith that produces no obedience. They are saying the same thing from different angles: saving faith is a faith that *acts*.

James makes this vivid:

— James 2:19

The demons believe. They know exactly who God is. They know Jesus is the Son of God — they said so to His face (Mark 5:7). Their belief is accurate, complete, and utterly useless — because it produces no obedience. Faith that does not obey is not saving faith. It is dead faith:

*"For just as the body without the spirit is dead, so also
faith without works is dead."*

— James 2:26

Belief matters. Belief is essential. But belief that refuses to obey the command Jesus Himself gave — to be baptized — is not the faith that saves. It is the faith of demons.

.   .   .

"What About the Thief on the Cross?"

This is the last refuge of the argument against baptism. "The thief on the cross was saved without being baptized."

The thief on the cross received his promise from Jesus while Jesus was still alive. And that matters — more than most people realize. The writer of Hebrews explains:

— Hebrews 9:16–17

A will — a testament — does not go into effect while the person who made it is still living. You do not inherit under a will while the testator is alive. The New Testament — the new covenant, the new will — was not in force while Jesus lived. It went into effect at His death.

The thief lived under the old covenant. Jesus, while He walked the earth, had authority to forgive sins directly (Matthew 9:6) — and He exercised that authority with the thief. The thief is not an example of how people are saved under the new covenant. He is an example of Jesus' personal authority exercised under the old one.

Your template is not the thief. Your template is Acts 2 — Peter preaching under the new covenant and telling people to repent and be baptized for the forgiveness of their sins. Your template is Acts 22:16 — Ananias telling Saul to be baptized and wash away his sins. Your template is Romans 6 — buried with Christ and raised to walk in newness of life.

Why Do You Delay?

Every command of Jesus points to it. Every sermon the apostles preached includes it. Every letter they wrote affirms it. Every conversion in the book of Acts demonstrates it. The one time "faith alone" appears in Scripture, it says "not by faith alone." The one time an apostle directly addresses whether baptism saves, he says, "Baptism now saves you."

Is baptism really necessary?

Every Scripture says it is.

And Ananias, when he came to a man who had already seen the risen Lord, who had already believed, who had already fasted and prayed for three days — Ananias did not say, "You are already saved." He said:

> *"Now why do you delay? Get up and be baptized, and wash away your sins, calling on His name."*
> — Acts 22:16

The question is not whether baptism is necessary. The question is the one Ananias asked two thousand years ago — the same question that echoes through every page of the New Testament, through every conversion account, through every apostolic letter:

Why do you delay?

Scripture Index

2 Kings

5:1–14

Matthew

3:16 • 9:6 • 16:18 • 28:19–20

Mark

5:7 • 16:16

John

3:3, 5, 23

Acts

2:6–8, 37–47 • 8:12–13, 35–39 • 9:1–18

10:44–48 • 11:15 • 16:14–15, 30–33

18:8 • 19:1–5 • 22:16

Romans

6:3–4

1 Corinthians

1:12–17 • 12:13

Galatians

2:16 • 3:27

Ephesians

1:3 • 2:8–9 • 4:5

Colossians

1:13 • 2:12

Titus

3:5

Hebrews

9:16–17 • 11:7, 30

James

2:19, 24, 26

1 Peter

3:21

1 John

3:4

Notes

Notes

More from NobleMind Press

All titles available free at **noblemind.study**
Print editions available wherever books are sold.

A New and Living Way

What the Bible Teaches About Prayer

Bridge Moments

Making the Most of Every Opportunity

Change the Mind, Change the Man

Inspired by the teaching of Freddie Anderson

One Day Closer to Home

A Book of Hope for Those in the Final Chapters

The Character No One Could Invent

A deep look at the character of Jesus Christ

The God Who Showed Up

What His Names Reveal About Who He Is

Through the Valley

What God Says When the Shadow Is Real

Your Name Means Everything: A Good Name

A Straight-Talk Guide for Young Men Who Want to Matter

Your Name Means Everything: Strength and Dignity

What the Bible Says to Young Women About Character, Wisdom, and Faith

www.ingramcontent.com/pod-product-compliance
Lightning Source LLC
Chambersburg PA
CBHW020519160726
47991CB00007B/3021